The Seed I Planted

Mick Manning
and Brita Granström

W
FRANKLIN WATTS
LONDON·SYDNEY

For Charles Desmond Manning

First published in 2002
by Franklin Watts,
96 Leonard Street,
London EC2A 4XD

Franklin Watts Australia
45-51 Huntley Street
Alexandria
NSW 2015

The illustrations in this book
have been drawn by both Brita and Mick

Text and illustrations © 2002 Mick Manning
and Brita Granström
Series editor: Rachel Cooke
Art director: Jonathan Hair

Printed in Hong Kong, China
A CIP catalogue record is available from
the British Library.
Dewey Classification 582
ISBN 0 7496 4301 3 (hbk)
ISBN 0 7496 4789 2 (pbk)

Contents

Conker-hunting   6

Autumn winds   14

Planting time   18

Growing   20

From sapling to tree   24

Thirty years later   26

Seed ideas   28

Seed words and index   30

Conker-hunting

I've always loved conkers. When I was a boy, I'd go conker-hunting with my dad.

Conkers are the seeds of the Horse chestnut tree.

conkers

Horse chestnut leaf

A seed is a tough-cased package that contains a new plant and all the food it needs to start growing.

We'd kick up dead
leaves, give low
branches a shake.
We'd even ask
a passing squirrel.

Seeds come in lots of shapes
and sizes – from tiny grains
to big nuts. Some seeds
come in soft fruits.
Conkers come
in spiky jackets!

Fallen conkers find good hiding places!

To grow properly, seeds need to travel away from their parent plant.

They roll and bounce.
They can even float.

Some fruits are eaten by birds.
The seeds inside are
'plopped out' later!

Some seeds fall into
water and float away
downstream.

11

All good conker hunters know that the sticks you throw get stuck - until the wind works them loose!

People have always used sticks to collect seeds, fruit and nuts. You have to be careful not to hit yourself, though!

12

Autumn winds

One autumn there
was a terrific gale.
I fell asleep listening
to the wind, and the
trees creaking . . .

Many plants – from huge
trees to dandelions – rely
on autumn winds to shake
their seeds free.

14

16

Next morning Dad woke me early. Pocketfuls and pocketfuls of spiky conkers lay among the fallen leaves.

We don't hunt conkers for food – but there are lots of seeds and fruits we can gather in the autumn to eat, such as hazelnuts and blackberries. Birds, squirrels and mice like to eat them, too.

Planting time

I planted my best conker.
I watered and
waited. And
watered and
waited . . .

Before it can start to grow, a conker needs
some time in warm, damp, dark soil.

Growing

And one day it
began to grow.

First came a
root, then a
green shoot.

Later, two tiny
conker leaves
unfurled.

*Roots take in water
and 'goodness' from
the soil.*

The shoot
pushes up out
of the soil.

The first leaves to
grow are called the
seed leaves.

21

A young tree is called a sapling.

Spring came. Dad scattered some seeds, and I planted out my sapling in a sheltered spot.

Spring is the best time to sow seeds and plant out saplings. The spring sunshine helps them grow.

Once a plant has its green leaves, it can make its own food with them by using energy from sunlight.

From sapling to tree

Over the years,
I watched it
grow . . .
  and grow . . .
    and grow . . .

Some plants grow from a seed, flower and die in just a year. Some trees take a hundred years or more to grow.

*Winter,
2 years later*

Spring,
8 years later

Summer,
20 years later

25

Thirty years later

And I grew too!
Look! The seed
I planted has
become an
enormous tree.

Come on!
Let's go conker-
hunting . . .

27

Seed ideas

Find out some more about seeds - and play with conkers!

Plant a bean

Unlike conkers, beans grow quickly.

1. Line a jam jar with blotting paper and fill the jar inside it with damp cotton wool.
2. Push some broad beans between the glass and blotting paper.
3. Keep the jar in a dark place and check it each day. Don't let the cotton wool dry out.

Conker fun

Make some conker animals - or just play conkers!

matchsticks

string

Look at some seeds

Discover more about how seeds move around. Here are some examples:

Some stick to fur - until they are scratched off!

Some shoot out when their seed pod explodes.

Some plants shake out their seeds like pepper from a pepper pot.

Some seeds spin from their parent trees on wings like helicopters.

Some seeds are eaten by wildlife . . .

. . . and some are buried and forgotten!

Seed words and index

flower We say a plant flowers when it grows flowers. Flowers are where a plant's seeds are made. Page 24

food All living things need food. Plants make their own food in their leaves. Pages 6, 17, 23

fruit A protective layer that surrounds the seeds of some plants. Some fruits are good to eat, others are poisonous. An apple is a fruit and the pips are the seeds. Pages 9, 11, 12, 17

grain A type of seed, usually very small, produced by plants such as wheat or rice. Page 9

leaf The part of the plant, usually green, where the plant makes its food. The first leaves plants grow are their seed leaves. Pages 6, 17, 20, 21, 23

nut A fruit or seed with a hard, dry 'shell'. Pages 9, 12

parent plant The plant that a seed came from. Page 10

roots The parts of a plant, usually under the ground, which hold it steady and take in water and goodness from the soil. Page 20

sapling A young tree. Pages 22, 23, 24

seed A tough-cased package produced by plants which contains a new plant and a store of food to help it start growing. Pages 6, 9, 10, 11, 12, 14, 17, 23, 24, 26

stem Part of a plant that connects its other parts together, such as the roots and the leaves. Pages 20, 21